Imagine That! Stories

Visualizing and Verbalizing®
For Language Comprehension and Thinking

GRADE

A Nanci Bell Book

COPYRIGHT © 2007 Nanci Bell
Gander Publishing
412 Higuera Street, Suite 200
San Luis Obispo, CA 93401
805-541-5523 • 800-554-1819
ISBN 0-945856-60-1
978-0-945856-60-3

VISUALIZING AND VERBALIZING AND V/V ARE REGISTERED
TRADEMARKS OF NANCI BELL.

13 12 11 10   3 4 5 6

All rights reserved. No part of this material shall be reproduced or transmitted in any form or by any means, electronic or mechanical, including photocopying, recording, or by any information or retrieval systems, without prior written permission from the Publisher. Printed in the U.S.A.

Directions	iv
Sentence by Sentence	1
Multiple Sentence	17
Whole Paragraph	25
Paragraph by Paragraph	33

Introduction:

The mysterious, the unusual, the unexplained... Imagery is the medium through which language that describes our diverse world is revealed in all its detail and complexity.

The *Imagine That!* series provides nonfiction stories with which to practice building imagery for oral and written language comprehension. These challenging, high-imagery stories introduce true and unusual topics for students to visualize, including natural disasters, legends, unique animals, odd plants, mysteries, fascinating phenomena, and people of great achievement. Each story is presented in language appropriate to the grade level, and the content is sure to capture the interest of students and instructors alike.

The mysteries of the world are waiting. Let's fly.

Nanci Bell
2007

How to Use *Imagine That! Stories*:

The *Imagine That! Stories* can be used with any program of instruction to develop imagery for language comprehension, and they can also be used specifically with the *Visualizing and Verbalizing*® (V/V®) program. These stories give students practice visualizing the big picture, the gestalt, and should be used when doing the steps that develop concept imagery as a base for critical thinking.

While the stories have been arranged in sections that align with specific steps of V/V®, all *Imagine That! Stories* can be used with any of the following V/V® steps:

- Sentence by Sentence
- Sentence by Sentence with Higher Order Thinking (HOT)
- Multiple Sentence with HOT
- Whole Paragraph with HOT
- Paragraph by Paragraph with HOT
- Whole Page with HOT

Tips:

- **Story Arrangement**
  Although all the stories in this volume are written at a second-grade reading level, within each section, stories have been sequentially ordered to increase in conceptual difficulty.

- **Illustrations**
  Illustrations have been provided for stories that contain unfamiliar subjects. These images can be presented to the students before the paragraph is read, to help them build their own imagery.

- **Topic Sentences**
  You may find that the first sentence of a paragraph introduces a general topic to be imaged, and the rest of the paragraph goes on to describe detailed imagery for the topic. For example, in the story "A Secret Message Drop," the first line reads, "Spies use a dead drop—a secret way to pass messages—when they want to stay hidden." While the sentence contains concrete detail that can be imaged, such as the spies and their messages, the sentence also contains some concepts that require further information. For example, this sentence does not tell us what the dead drop method is, or how the spies stay hidden. When working with students, it is appropriate to have them leave that portion of their image indistinct. You may explain to the students that the rest of the paragraph will fill in the blanks in their imagery.

- **Higher Order Thinking (HOT) Questions**
  The stories are followed by main idea, inference, conclusion, evaluation, and prediction questions. The order of these HOT questions is such that they stimulate students' thinking first about the gestalt and then about the details of the story. In some questions, key words are italicized to indicate emphasis. Also, contrast questions are included to stimulate and guide the students' critical reasoning. Finally, in some instances, the HOT questions introduce additional information, from which the students can extend their thinking about the story.

Sentence by Sentence

1   A Sticky Place

Bubblegum Alley, a thin street between two buildings, is a strange and smelly place. Its walls are covered top to bottom with wads of chewed gum. Some sticky globs are stretched to make shapes and pictures. A few wads even spell out people's names.

> From what you pictured…
> What is the main idea of the story?
> Why do you think this alley is *strange*?
> Why do you think someone would make shapes with their gum?
> Do you think many people visit this alley? Why or why not?
> Do you think people ever try to clean the walls of this alley? Why or why not?
> Would you leave your gum on the wall of Bubblegum Alley? Why or why not?

2   Surfing Dolphins

Dolphins often play by swimming near a ship. As the ship moves through the water, it makes a wave in front of its bow. Dolphins ride the wave, letting it push them along. People on the deck of the ship watch the dolphins leap and play.

> From what you pictured…
> What is the main idea of this story?
> Why do you think dolphins ride the bow waves of ships?
> Why do you think the dolphins swim in *front* of the ship and not behind it?
> Why do you think people on the ship watch the dolphins?
> Do you think a dolphin could ride the wave in front of a small rowboat? Why or why not?

3 Dessert on a Stick

Some people eat fried Twinkies® on a stick. First they put the sweet treat on a stick and freeze it. Then they cover the treat with batter and dip it in hot oil to cook it. People bite through the crust to get to the gooey filling inside.

> From what you pictured…
> What is the main idea of this story?
> Why do you think people eat the fried Twinkies®?
> Why do you think they put the treat on a stick *before* they freeze it? Why not after?
> Why do you think they cover the treat in batter before they fry it?
> Why do you think the filling is *gooey* by the end and not still frozen?

4 A Great Slide

Alongside the Great Wall of China, people ride sleds down a long metal slide. In one place, the wall runs over a tall hill. People hike up the wall's stone steps to the top of the hill. Then they sit on a wheeled sled and speed all the way down the slide.

> From what you pictured…
> What is the main idea of this story?
> Why do you think people ride down the slide?
> Why do you think people hike to the top of the hill?
> Why do you think the sled has wheels?
> How do you think people get down the hill if they don't ride the slide?

Twinkies® Continental Baking Company

5   Shipwreck Homes

Some people in Denmark build homes out of wood from old shipwrecks. For years, ships have crashed onto the rocky shore. People gather wood from the old wrecks on the beach and use it for beams in their homes. Then they cover their roofs with dried seaweed.

> From what you pictured…
> What is the main idea of this story?
> Do you think using wood from the shipwrecks is a good idea? Why or why not?
> Why do you think so many ships have crashed on the shore?
> Why do you think the people use *dry* seaweed? Why not wet seaweed?
> What might people do if they run out of wood from shipwrecks?

6   Dolphin to the Rescue

One dolphin saved a boy from drowning in the sea. A large wave had swept the boy off his boat and into the water. The dolphin swam beneath the boy and pushed him up for air. The boy's father pulled him back onto the boat.

> From what you pictured…
> What is the main idea of this story?
> Why do you think the dolphin helped the boy?
> What might have happened if the dolphin hadn't helped the boy?
> How do you think the boy felt when the dolphin pushed him up for air?
> What do you think happened after the boy's father pulled him onto the boat?

7 Tied-Up Ox

A farmer might tie his ox to a clump of grass instead of a tree. Sometimes an ox gets scared and thrashes back and forth. If tied to a strong tree, he will hurt himself while trying to get free. But the ox can yank the grass out of the ground and not get hurt.

> From what you pictured…
> What is the main idea of this story?
> Why do you think a farmer would tie up his ox?
> Why do you think the ox gets scared?
> Do you think the ox stops thrashing once he hurts himself? Why or why not?
> Why do you think the ox hurts himself when tied to a *tree* but not grass?

8 Storm Counting

Some kids stay calm during a storm by counting. They start to count when they see a bolt of lightning flash across the sky. They stop counting once they hear the boom of thunder. If the kids count higher than five, the lightning was far away.

> From what you pictured…
> What is the main idea of this story?
> Why might the kids want to stay calm during a storm?
> Why do you think the counting helps the kids stay calm?
> Do you think the kids want to count for a short or long time? Explain.
> What do you think it means if the kids count to less than five? Do you think the storm is close or far away? Explain.

9 Argentine Cactus Moth

One moth lays her eggs on the flat pad of a cactus plant. She stacks her eggs so they stick up like a long spine. When the eggs hatch, small worm-like larvae burrow into the pad. They eat the inside of the pad till it is hollow.

> From what you pictured…
> What is the main idea of this story?
> Why do you think the moth lays her eggs on the cactus? Why not on a rock?
> Why do you think she stacks her eggs to look like a spine?
> The outside skin of a cactus is tough, but the inside is soft. Why do you think the larvae burrow into the cactus pad?
> Do you think the larvae help or hurt the cactus? Explain.

10 Grass Roofs

Some homes in Norway have grass growing in dirt on their roofs. In the winter, these thick lawns trap warm air in the house. When it rains, the dirt soaks up the water before it leaks through the roof. The people who live in these homes put goats on their roofs to eat the grass when it grows too long.

> From what you pictured…
> What is the main idea of this story?
> What do you think would happen to one of these homes if it rained too much?
> What do you think would happen if the people let the grass keep growing?
> Do you think the people let the goats eat *all* the grass? Why or why not?
> Do you think these people *water* their roofs? Why or why not?

11 Kea Parrots

Kea parrots live in the hills of New Zealand. They often visit campsites there. The campers take pictures of the birds hopping on the ground. But sometimes the birds chew on car tires and steal food. Then people get mad and chase the keas away.

> From what you pictured…
> What is the main idea of this story?
> Do you think kea parrots are afraid of people? Why or why not?
> Do you think these campers like the keas? Why or why not?
> Why do you think the birds chew on the car tires?
> What might the campers do if the keas come back?

12   A Secret Message Drop

Spies use a dead drop—a secret way to pass messages—when they want to stay hidden. A spy puts a note under a rock, in a book, or in a tree hole. He marks the spot with chalk or chewed gum. Later another spy sees the mark and finds the note. Then he hurries off before people notice him.

From what you pictured...

What is the main idea of this story?

Why do you think this way of passing messages is called the "dead drop"?

Why do you think the spies would want to stay hidden?

Why do you think the first spy marked the note's spot?

Why would chewed gum be a good thing to mark a note's spot with?

Do you think the spy would let other people see him leave notes? Why or why not?

What do you think would happen if the two spies saw each other?

13   Tree Bark Makeup

Some women in Asia make face lotion from tree bark. They peel the bark off a tree and grind it up on a wet piece of stone. They mash the bark until it turns into a yellow paste that smells nice. The women rub the paste on their cheeks and noses. They think it makes their skin smooth and pretty.

From what you pictured...

What is the main idea of this story?

Why do you think the women grind the bark on a *wet* piece of stone? Why not a dry one?

Do you think it is hard to make the paste? Why or why not?

Why do you think the women want to wear the paste?

Do you think the women would still wear the paste if it didn't smell nice? Why or why not?

Do you think men wear the paste, too? Why or why not?

14   A Fishy Snack

Young men once held contests to see who could eat the most live goldfish. One by one, they grabbed the wiggling fish from a tank. They dropped the fish in their mouths and swallowed. A crowd cringed as each man gulped as many fish as he could. Some men ate too many fish and got sick.

> From what you pictured…
> What is the main idea of the story?
> Why do you think someone would want to win a goldfish-eating contest?
> Do you think it was difficult to win a goldfish-eating contest? Why or why not?
> Why do you think people wanted to watch these contests?
> Would you like to compete in a goldfish-eating contest? Why or why not?

15   Bad Habit

In one zoo, a chimp named Charlie has a bad habit: he smokes. Charlie first smoked when a man threw a lit cigarette into his pen. Now he begs other smokers for cigarettes as they walk by. Zookeepers warn people not to give cigarettes to the chimp. If he keeps smoking, he will get very sick.

> From what you pictured…
> What is the main idea of this story?
> Why do you think smoking is a bad habit for Charlie?
> How do you think Charlie learned to smoke?
> Why do you think the man threw the cigarette into Charlie's pen?
> Why do you think Charlie *begs* for cigarettes from other smokers?
> What do you think the zookeepers might do if they saw someone throw a cigarette to Charlie?

16   Worms for Dinner

For dinner in Korea, a cook might serve a hot dish of silkworms. The cook first pulls the fat worms from their silk cocoons and boils them. Then he soaks some of the worms in a salty brown sauce. He fries others to a crisp in a pan of hot oil. Then he serves the steaming hot worms on plates with rice.

>From what you pictured...
> What is the main idea of this story?
> Why do you think the cook first pulls the worms from their cocoons? Why not boil the cocoons, too?
> Why do you think the cook soaks the worms in a salty sauce?
> Do you think people also eat uncooked silkworms? Why or why not?
> Would you like to eat silkworms? Why or why not?

17   Rain Forest Medicine

In a rain forest tribe, a doctor called a *shaman* treats sick people with plants. He hikes up a steep trail through the trees. He carries a shovel and a sack on his back. When he sees a brown root sticking out of the ground, he digs it up and puts it in the sack. He takes the root back to his hut, chops it up, and feeds it to a sick patient.

>From what you pictured...
> What is the main idea of this story?
> Why do you think the doctor uses *plants* to treat sick people? Why not pills?
> Do you think he uses every plant in the forest or just some? Explain.
> Why do you think he chops up the root?
> What do you think happens to the patient after she eats the root?

18 Spitting Llama

A llama spits at other llamas when they try to steal his food. First, as a warning, he pulls his ears back and tilts his nose up. If the llamas ignore him, he throws up in his mouth. Then he spits out the stinky green glob, which sticks in their fur. The glob's stench scares them off.

> From what you pictured…
> What is the main idea of this story?
> Why do you think the llama *spits* when other llamas try to steal his food? Why not bite or kick?
> Why do you think the llama warns the others before he spits?
> Why do you think the llama's spit smells so bad?
> What do you think would happen if the other llamas still did not go away?

19 Couch's Spadefoot Toad

A Couch's spadefoot toad burrows a hole in dry desert ground and sleeps for a long time. He wakes up when it rains and water soaks into the ground. Then he digs out of his hole and hops in a fresh puddle. He hunts small beetles, ants, and other bugs. When the ground dries out, the toad digs a new hole and goes back to sleep.

> From what you pictured…
> What is the main idea of this story?
> Why do you think the toad buries himself?
> Why do you think the toad digs out of his hole when it rains?
> Why do you think the toad hunts bugs?
> Do you think the toad sleeps a lot? Why or why not?

20   President Arrested

When Franklin Pierce was president long ago, he was arrested. On a dark night, Pierce was racing his horse through town. A woman stepped in front of him without looking and he ran right over her. The sheriff came and took Pierce to jail. But when Pierce told his story, the sheriff let him go.

From what you pictured…

What is the main idea of the story?

Why do you think the sheriff took President Pierce to jail?

Why do you think the sheriff let Pierce go?

Do you think President Pierce could have avoided the accident? Why or why not?

How do you think President Pierce felt about getting arrested?

21   Floating Farms

The people of Inle Lake grow crops on floating farms. First, men in boats throw dead plants on top of the water until they make a mound. They push the mounds into rows and pin them to the lake floor with wood poles. Then they plant seeds for their crops in the mounds. Months later, they float beside the rows and pick vegetables from the tall crops.

From what you pictured…

What is the main idea of this story?

Why do you think the crops grow on mounds of dead plants? Why not just on the water?

Why do you think the men push the mounds into rows?

What might happen if a farmer forgot to pin a mound to the lake floor?

What do you think the farmers will do with the crops when they die?

SENTENCE BY SENTENCE

22 Sniffing Kiwi Bird

The kiwi bird is a unique bird that sniffs out his food. He has nostrils on the tip of his long thin beak. He searches the forest floor at night, poking his beak into the soil to sniff. He plucks out worms and bugs hiding deep in the dirt. When he smells ripe berries on the ground, he eats those up, too.

> From what you pictured…
> What is the main idea of this story?
> Why do you think the kiwi *sniffs out* his food instead of *looking* for it?
> How do you think it helps the kiwi to have his nostrils at the *tip* of his beak?
> Why do you think the kiwi's beak is so long and thin?
> Why do you think he sniffs in the soil?

23 Stuffed Fish Sham

One fisherman fooled his town when he claimed he caught the largest bass ever. The man reeled the large fish in from a river and took it home. He stuffed the fish with lead weights and brought it back to a river dock. People cheered as the man weighed the fish on a scale. The stuffed fish weighed more than nine pounds, a state record!

From what you pictured…

What is the main idea of this story?

What do you think happened to the man next?

Why do you think the man wanted to fool his town?

Why do you think the man took the fish home before weighing it?

Why do you think the man stuffed the fish with lead weights? Why not with feathers?

Why do you think the people cheered?

How do you think someone could have found out that the man was cheating?

24 Watch Out For Falling Bricks!

Bricks keep popping out of the walls of old Fort Jefferson. The fort, which sits on a small island, has tall brick walls lined with iron window frames. When it rains, rust grows on the wet frames. As the rust builds up, it slowly pushes on nearby bricks. Sometimes chunks of the brick wall suddenly pop off and fall to the ground.

From what you pictured…

What is the main idea of this story?

Do you think it is safe to visit Fort Jefferson? Why or why not?

What might happen to the fort if the falling brick problem is not fixed?

Do you think bricks would fall if the window frames were made out of wood? Why or why not?

What might people do to stop the bricks from falling?

25   Tiny Bones

The smallest human bones are deep in our ears. These bones are named after their shapes: the hammer, the anvil, and the stirrup. Sound waves go in the ear and bounce off the hammer. Then the hammer bangs on the anvil, which shakes the stirrup back and forth. When these bones move, we hear sounds.

> From what you pictured…
>
> What is the main idea of this story?
>
> Do you think the bones move and shake more with loud sounds or soft sounds? Explain.
>
> What might happen if you broke one of these bones?
>
> All together, these bones are smaller than a dime. Why do you think these bones are so small?
>
> Why do you think the bones are *deep* in our ears?

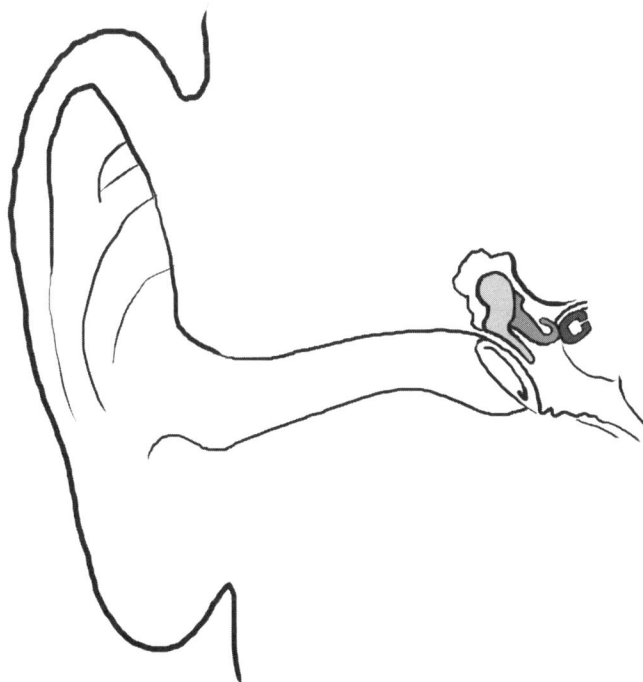

Sentence by Sentence

Multiple Sentence

26 Crater of Diamonds State Park

People visit one state park to dig for gems. There they walk through a large dirt field. They scoop the dirt onto wire screens. Then they shake the screens to sift out rocks. Each day someone finds a small white, brown, or yellow diamond. People get to keep the stones they find. Some sell their gems for thousands of dollars.

> From what you pictured...
> What is the main idea of this story?
> Why do you think people come to this state park?
> Why do you think the guests use the wire screens? Why not just use their fingers?
> What might someone do if they found a diamond? Explain.
> Do you think there are many places where people can dig up and *keep* diamonds? Why or why not?

27 Crocodile Bird

It is said there is a kind of bird that is safe in the mouth of a crocodile. This bird lives near a river where crocs sun themselves on the banks. Sometimes a croc will open his jaws wide. Then this bird flies down and hops inside the croc's mouth. The bird picks bits of rotting food from between the croc's teeth and eats them. When the croc's teeth are clean, the bird flies off unharmed.

> From what you pictured...
> What is the main idea of this story?
> Why do you think the crocodile does not eat the bird?
> Do you think *any* bird could do this, or just the crocodile bird? Explain
> Do you think this bird is afraid of crocodiles? Why or why not?
> Why do you think the crocodile opens his jaws *wide*?

28 Singing Finch

A young zebra finch sings while he sleeps. During the day, the baby bird sits in his nest by his father. He listens while his father calls out to his mother in song. When the young bird naps, he practices the songs he has heard. He also sings every night while he sleeps. Soon the finch learns the tune, and sings while he is awake.

> From what you pictured…
> What is the main idea of this story?
> Why do you think the baby bird listens to his father sing?
> Why do you think the young finch practices singing while he sleeps? Why not while he is awake?
> Why do you think the baby bird sings *every* night while he sleeps?

29 Bajau Seaweed Farmers

There is a group of people that farms seaweed in the ocean. They live in huts that stand on stilts in shallow water. Each day men climb down from their huts to their boats. They paddle out to their floating beds of seaweed. When they reach a bed, they cut off many long leaves. They take the leaves home to dry and serve them with fish at meals.

> From what you pictured…
> What is the main idea of this story?
> Why do you think the Bajau huts need to be on *stilts*?
> Why do you think the men need their boats?
> Why do think it is important for the bed of seaweed to be floating?
> Why do you think the men dry the seaweed leaves before serving them?

30 Hair Wars

Hair Wars is a fashion show for wild wigs. Models wear the large wigs and strut down a runway. Some wigs stand five feet above a model's head. Many wigs have parts that move. One wig had a live snake crawl out the top. Another wig had two dragons made of braids that blew smoke. A toy plane took off from the top of a third wig and flew over the cheering crowd.

From what you pictured…

What is the main idea of the story?

Why do you think the show is called *Hair Wars*?

Do you think it might be difficult to wear one of these wigs? Why or why not?

Do you think it was dangerous for the model to have a snake in her wig? Why or why not?

Why do you think the crowd was cheering?

Would you want to watch a fashion show like this? Why or why not?

31   Carousel Training

Long ago, knights rode a carousel to train for battle. Each knight sat on a wooden horse that dangled by a chain from a beam. The beams stuck out from a central pole set in the ground. Servants hung large metal rings from trees around the carousel. Then they handed each knight a long lance. The servants pushed the carousel in a circle. As the knights spun around, they tried to poke their lances through the rings.

> From what you pictured…
>
> What is the main idea of this story?
>
> Why do you think the carousel had *wooden* horses? Why not real ones?
>
> Why do you think they *hung* the rings from the trees? Why not *nail* them?
>
> Do you think it was hard for the knights to poke the tips of their lances through the rings? Why or why not?
>
> People now ride carousels for fun at carnivals and theme parks. Why do you think carousels are no longer used to train knights?

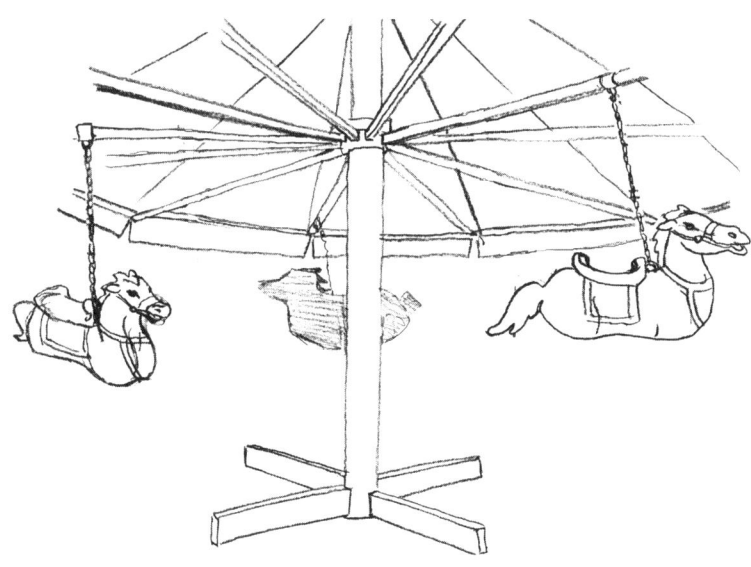

32   The Russian Ice Slide

Long ago, people rode down a big icy slide. This slide had a tall staircase that led up to a wide platform. A steep wooden ramp sloped down off the platform. In winter, workers stood on the platform and poured water down the ramp. The water froze into a thick layer of ice. Riders carried sleds up to the top of the slide. Then they sat on their sleds and raced down the icy ramp.

From what you pictured…

What is the main idea of this story?

Why do you think people sat on *sleds* to slide down? Why not just sit on the ice itself?

Do you think this slide was dangerous? Why or why not?

Do you think people rode the slide when the weather got warmer in spring? Why or why not?

Why do you think the slide needed a staircase? Why not walk up the ramp?

33   The Mighty Tongue

The tongue is a strong muscle that moves a lot. It can move up, down, and side-to-side. Some people can even curl their tongues in the shape of the capital letter U. When you eat, the tongue moves food around in your mouth. Tiny bumps on your tongue called taste buds help you taste the food. The tongue also moves when you speak. Sometimes you tap the tip of your tongue on the roof of your mouth when you say words.

From what you pictured…

What is the main idea of this story?

Why do you think the tongue has to move so much?

Why do you think the tongue needs to move food around in the mouth?

What might happen if you didn't have any taste buds?

Do you think someone could still speak if he couldn't move his tongue? Why or why not?

MULTIPLE SENTENCE

34   Monkey Mail

Sea monkeys are a kind of small shrimp some kids keep as pets. Tiny dry eggs come through the mail in a box. Kids soak the eggs in water for a day. Once the eggs hatch, the sea monkeys are each the size of the period at the end of this sentence. They soon grow three eyes, many legs, and thin tails. In the next few weeks, they grow to half an inch long. They beat their legs to swim around their small plastic tank.

> From what you pictured…
> What is the main idea of the story?
> Why do you think the kids might want sea monkeys as pets?
> Why do you think the eggs have to be soaked in water for a day?
> Do you think the sea monkey eggs ever hatch in the mail? Why or why not?
> Why do you think these creatures might be called *sea monkeys*?
> Would you want to have sea monkeys as pets?

35   Rotten Sneaker Contest

The Rotten Sneaker Contest is held each year. Kids from all over the U.S. compete to see whose shoes stink the worst. Some kids bring their shoes in sealed bags. Brave judges sniff the insides of each pair. The smellier the shoes, the higher they score them. They also give points for torn laces and holes in the toes. Every year they add the winning pair to the *Hall of Fumes*, for all to see. The winner receives $500 and a new pair of shoes.

> From what you pictured…
> What is the main idea of the story?
> Why do you think kids want to compete in this contest?
> Why do you think some kids brought their shoes in *sealed* bags?
> Why do you think the story calls the judges "brave"?
> Would you want to be a judge for a rotten sneaker contest? Why or why not?
> Do you think the *Hall of Fumes* gets a lot of visitors? Why or why not?

Multiple Sentence

Whole Paragraph

WHOLE PARAGRAPH

36   In a Tight Space

A group of students once tried to stuff as many people as they could into a phone booth. The first people in stood straight up. Then more wedged in on their sides. Some went in headfirst. Others squeezed their feet and legs in first. People outside the booth helped push more students in. In the end, twenty-five people had crammed into the booth!

From what you pictured…

What is the main idea of the story?

Why do you think the students needed help getting into the booth?

Why do you think someone would squeeze their feet and legs in first instead of their head?

Do you think the students could still use the phone in the booth once it was full? Why or why not?

Do you think it was difficult for the people to get out of the booth? Why or why not?

37 Ghost Picture

People claim a ghost named the Brown Lady haunts a house in England. Many have seen this ghost glide toward them in a long brown dress. Her skin has a pale glow and she often holds a lantern. A reporter once came to the house to take pictures. Just after sunset, he saw the ghost on the stairs. He quickly snapped a picture. The photo showed the ghost staring back at the man.

> From what you pictured…
> What is the main idea of this story?
> How do you think the reporter felt when he saw the ghost?
> What do you think most people did when they saw the ghost?
> Why do you think the ghost often carried a lantern?
> What do you think the reporter did with the picture of the ghost?

38 Opal Homes

Some people live in old gem mines. Miners once drilled deep holes in the side of a mountain. They searched the holes for shiny stones called opals. When the miners left, people made the empty holes their homes. They set up tables, chairs, and beds inside. Then they hung pictures and lanterns on the rock walls. Some lucky people even found opals the miners had missed.

> From what you pictured…
> What is the main idea of this story?
> Why do you think people would want to live in those mines?
> Why do you think the miners left?
> Why do you think people are *lucky* if they find opals that the miners had missed?
> Would you like to live in one of these homes? Why or why not?

39   Lights Out in Iceland

One night in Iceland, a whole city turned off its lights. Street lamps, stoplights, and store signs went dark. People turned off lights in their homes, too. They lit small candles to walk outside. When they looked up at the dark sky, they saw thousands of stars.

>From what you pictured…
What is the main idea of this story?
Why do you think the city turned off all its lights?
Do you think people saw more or less stars with the lights off? Why?
Why do you think people needed to light small candles?
Why do you think people lit small candles and not big flashlights?

40   Tasty Clothes

In one village, cows sometimes eat people's clothes. The villagers wash their clothes with soap that tastes good to the cows. When the clothes are clean, people hang them over a fence to dry. Passing cows often chew on the clothes. Some even snatch the clothes right off the fence and enjoy the tasty snack.

>From what you pictured…
What is the main idea of this story?
What do you think the villagers do when they see a cow eating their clothes?
What do you think the villagers could do to keep the cows from eating the clothes?
Do you think clothes are good for the cows to eat? Why or why not?
Do you think these cows eat *dirty* clothes? Why or why not?

41 A Judge's Hidden Eyes

Long ago, a judge in China wore dark glasses in court. He hid his eyes behind two dark crystals. He wore the glasses while he listened to people argue. They could not see if his eyes looked happy or sad. Then the judge took off his glasses and told the people who was right.

> From what you pictured…
>
> What is the main idea of this story?
>
> Why do you think the judges used *dark* crystals? Why not clear ones?
>
> Why might the judge want to hide his eyes?
>
> Do you think people would argue differently if they could see his eyes? Explain.
>
> Why do you think the judge took off the glasses at the end?

42 Mermaid's Purse

One shark lays an egg in a small sac called a mermaid's purse. The thin pouch has two long threads on each end. These threads wedge between rocks, which keep the sac from floating away. Soon the egg hatches and a young shark swims out of the pouch. But if the threads lose their grip, waves will wash the sac up on a beach, and the egg will die.

From what you pictured…
What is the main idea of this story?
Why do you think the sac is called a mermaid's purse?
Why do you think the threads are *long*? Why not short?
Why do you think the eggs die if they wash onto the beach?
What might happen to the egg if the shark did not lay it in a pouch?

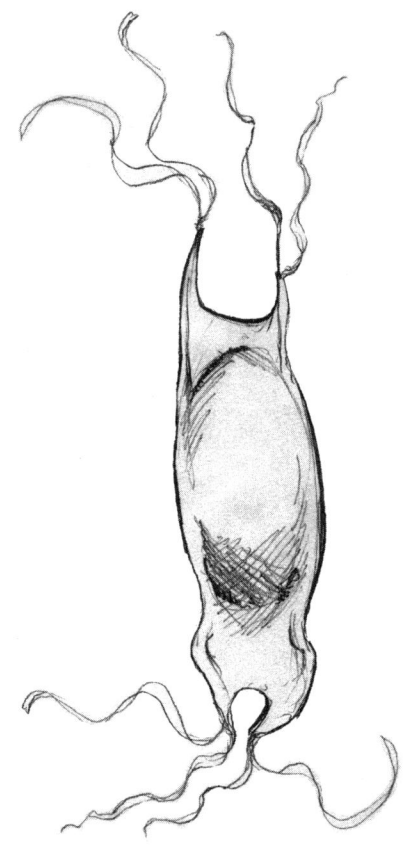

43 Jai Alai

Jai alai is a dangerous game to play. Four men stand on a long court facing a tall wall. Each man wears a helmet and straps a long scoop to his right hand. To begin the game, one man uses his scoop to fling and bounce a small rubber ball off the wall. Another man must use his scoop to catch and sling the ball back again. Players can hurl the ball down the court as fast as a race car. If the ball hits a man, it can break his arm or leg.

From what you pictured…
What is the main idea of this story?
Why do you think the story calls this game "dangerous"?
Why do you think players must wear helmets?
What might happen if the courts were short instead of long?
Do you think the ball would be hard to catch? Why or why not?

44   One Helpful Worm

The earthworm helps plants grow by digging tunnels. He burrows in the dirt near the roots of a plant. When it rains, water seeps into the ground. It flows through the worm's tunnels and reaches the roots. Then the roots soak up as much water as they can. With the worm's help, the plant grows tall and full.

From what you pictured…

What is the main idea of this story?

Why do you think the earthworm digs tunnels?

What might happen to the plant if the worm stopped digging tunnels?

Do you think people like having worms in their gardens? Why or why not?

Do you think it is better to have many worms in a garden or just one? Explain.

Paragraph by Paragraph

45 Seashell Houses

In one island village, people once lived in homes made of straw. But they cooked over open fires inside these homes. Sometimes sparks from the flames set the walls on fire. The homes burned down to the ground. The villagers rebuilt them, but the homes caught fire again. After a while, they grew tired of rebuilding their homes.

The villagers began to make their walls with white seashells instead of straw. They often ate clams and then threw the shells on the ground. Piles of shells covered the island. The villagers mixed the shells with mud and formed bricks. Then they laid the bricks in the sun to dry. They stacked the bricks to make solid walls for their new homes.

From what you pictured…

What is the main idea of this story?

Why do you think the seashell brick homes were better than the straw homes?

Do you think it was easier to build homes out of straw or shell bricks? Explain.

Why do you think the villagers mixed the shells with mud?

What do you think the villagers could have done to prevent their straw homes from burning down?

Do you think the villagers cooked over open fires in the new shell homes? Why or why not?

46   Pigeon Race

Some people enter their pet pigeons in a race. These birds can find their way home from faraway places. Each owner mails his bird in a wood crate to the race's starting point. There a race judge puts a numbered rubber band on each bird's leg. The race begins when the judge releases all the birds from their crates. He looks at his watch and writes down the time. The birds fly high in the sky back toward their homes.

Each owner uses a special clock in a locked box to time the bird's flight. When the bird arrives home, the owner slips the band off the bird's leg. He drops the band through a small slot in the top of the box. Then he turns a knob on the box's side to print the time on a slip of paper inside. All the owners bring their clocks to the judge. He unlocks the boxes to view the times. The bird with the fastest flight wins the race.

> From what you pictured…
>
> What is the main idea of this story?
>
> Why do you think people race their pet pigeons?
>
> Why do you think it is important that pigeons can find their way home from faraway places?
>
> Why do you think the rubber band is *numbered*?
>
> Why do you think the judge writes down the time when the birds first fly away?
>
> Why do you think the clock boxes are locked?
>
> Do you think the pigeons practice for the race? Why or why not?
>
> What do you think happens after a pigeon wins a race?

47 A Woman's Best Friend

A cat set fire to the home of Jamie Hanson, a woman with one leg. One day the woman sat on her couch watching TV. Her dog sat on the floor nearby. Suddenly, her cat jumped on a table and toppled a lit candle. Fake plants on the table caught fire from the candle's flame. Startled by the fire, Jamie fell off the couch.

Jamie's well-trained dog helped her call the fire department. While lying on the floor, she told her dog to get the phone. The dog grabbed the phone with his teeth and brought it to her. As the fire grew, she dialed for help.

Then the dog helped Jamie get out of the house. First he fetched her fake leg off the table. She tried to put it on, but it was too hot. By now, the whole room had filled with flames and dark smoke. Jamie crawled on the ground as the dog led her outside.

> From what you pictured…
> What is the main idea of this story?
> What do you think happened next?
> What might have happened if Jamie's dog had not helped her?
> Why do you think the fake leg was too hot to put on?
> What might Jamie have done if she *could* have put her fake leg on?
> Why do you think she *crawled* outside?

48 Great White Shark on Display

The great white shark needs a lot of open water to swim in. A full-grown white shark is as long as a truck. She hunts seals, big tuna fish, and even other sharks. A scientist once captured a great white shark and put her in a glass tank. The scientist tried to feed the shark fish, but she refused to eat. She also kept bumping into the tank's walls. After a few days, the shark died.

One day a fisherman caught a young, smaller white shark in his net. He gave the shark to an aquarium. Workers at the aquarium put her in their biggest fish tank. Each day many people crowded around the tank to see the white shark. Other sharks swam in the tank as well. When the white shark came near them, they turned and swam away.

After a few months, the white shark grew too fierce to stay in the tank. She grew in size and began to attack the other sharks. So the workers caught her in a big net and lifted her out of the water. They put her in a small tank on a boat. Then they sailed far out to sea and let her go.

> From what you pictured...
> What is the main idea of this story?
> Why do you think the first great white shark died?
> Why do you think the workers put the young white shark in their *biggest* fish tank? Why not a smaller one?
> Why do you think so many people wanted to see the white shark?
> Why do you think the white shark attacked the other sharks?
> Why do you think the workers released the shark?
> What might have happened if the workers kept the shark in the aquarium?

49 Fairy Pictures

One day two young girls sat by a creek and drew fairies on paper. They colored in the fairies' short dresses and sparkling wings. In the drawings, the fairies danced and flew. The girls cut the fairies out of the paper. They taped pins to the base of each fairy. Then they stuck the pins in the ground so the fairies stood straight up.

The girls took pictures with the fairies. One girl posed by some fairies near a tree stump. The other girl sat in a field and acted like she was talking to a fairy. One of the girls showed the pictures to her parents. Her mother was convinced that the fairies were real. The mother brought the pictures to a local writer. He printed them in the town's magazine.

The town argued over the fairies. People held large meetings and studied the pictures. The wings in the pictures looked blurred. Some people thought the fairies were flying. But others claimed that the fairies were paper cutouts. They thought wind made the paper wings move. Many years passed before one of the girls told the truth.

From what you pictured…

What is the main idea of this story?

Why do you think the girls posed in the pictures with the fairies?

Why do you think the mother showed them to the writer?

Why do you think some people thought the photos were faked?

What do you think happened after one of the girls told the truth about the fairies?

Why do you think the girl told the truth *years later*? Why not right away?

50   The Giant Squid

Long ago, sailors told tales of a huge squid monster. This fierce beast had a large slimy head with two eyes, each the size of a soccer ball. Round suckers edged with sharp teeth lined the beast's eight arms. It also had two tentacles, each as long as a bus, with sharp hooks at the ends. Sailors claimed this beast could leap out of the water and grab hold of a large ship. It could pull the ship to the sea floor with one tug.

Today, scientists call this beast the giant squid. They have only seen a few alive. The squid lives along the sea floor. Sometimes it comes to the surface to chase prey, but not to sink ships. Scientists dive deep into the sea looking for it but have not found it. To learn more, they study dead squid that have washed up on the beach. They have also found squid parts inside the stomachs of whales.

One man is searching the sea for a baby giant squid. The baby squid is the size of a cricket and swims near the water's surface. It is easier to catch than an adult squid. The man drops mesh nets into the water. One of his nets once caught a baby squid, but it died before he could bring it back to shore. The man wants to take a live baby back to his lab. He plans to raise the squid in a large round tank.

> From what you pictured...
> What is the main idea of this story?
> Why do you think sailors called the giant squid a *monster*?
> Why do you think scientists have only seen a few giant squids alive?
> Why do you think a baby giant squid is easier to catch than an adult one?
> Why do you think the baby squid died before the man reached the shore?
> Do you think the man will be able to raise a giant squid in his tank? Why or why not?

51 Fire Investigator

Some dogs help firemen find out if someone started a fire on purpose. A person may use gasoline to start a fire since gas burns quickly and makes big flames. So a dog must first learn what gas smells like. A fireman lets the dog smell a cap full of gas. Then he gives the dog a tasty dog biscuit. Later the man puts small drops of gas in a sidewalk crack and on some stairs. If the dog finds the drops, he gets a treat.

The man takes the dog to a field that has small piles of sticks on the ground. Under one of the piles, the man hides a small cloth soaked in gas. The dog sniffs each pile and sits down when he comes to the one with the cloth. The man rewards the dog with a tasty snack.

Soon the dog is ready to work at a real fire station. When the bell rings, he jumps into the truck with the firemen. They pull up to a house filled with black smoke and flames. After the men put out the fire, the dog enters the home. He climbs slowly over the burnt wood.

The dog sniffs the ground as he explores each room. When he smells gas on a scorched piece of carpet, he sits down. A fireman pats the dog on the head and feeds him a treat. The dog points his nose toward the rubble. The fireman scoops it into a plastic bag and takes it to the police.

> From what you pictured…
> What is the main idea of this story?
> Why do you think the fireman gives the dog a treat when he smells the gas?
> What might happen if the dog does not find the drops of gas?
> Why do you think the man *hides* the cloth?
> Why do you think the dog walks *slowly* over the burnt wood?
> Why do you think the fireman takes the rubble to the police?

52 Robot Roach

Some scientists studied a cockroach to learn how it moved. The roach has a flat body and six long legs. He runs very fast and can jump high in the air. He can climb over rocks and straight up walls. He can also crawl through cracks and under doors.

The scientists filmed the roach doing many things. The bug crawled over balls of wax and up steep ramps. Then the scientists put the roach on a treadmill. They watched the bug's legs move as he ran. They viewed the film and wrote many notes.

The scientists made a backpack for the roach that controlled how he moved. They used a remote control to turn the bug to the left or right. They could even make him jump. But sometimes they could not control the roach. The bug ran into walls and fell off the side of a table.

Then the scientists made a robot that moves like a roach. The robot has six metals legs that bend. Rubber tubes stretch along each leg. Puffs of air shoot through the tubes and move the legs. The scientists put a small camera on the robot's head. Soon it will help find people trapped in rubble after an earthquake.

From what you pictured…

What is the main idea of this story?

Why do you think the scientists *filmed* the cockroach?

Why do you think the scientists wanted to make the cockroach jump?

Why do you think the backpack failed to control the cockroach?

Why do you think the scientists put a camera on the robot's head?

Currently, many robots have wheels instead of legs. Why might a cockroach-shaped robot be better?

53 We All Scream for Ice Cream!

Thousands of years ago, the rulers of Asia ate the first ice cream. The emperor sent his servants to gather snow from the mountains. They scooped it up into leather sacks. Then they raced back to the palace. They topped the snow with fruit. Back then, only the rich could afford to eat this treat.

Years later, people mixed snow with milk and salt. They shook the mixture in a jar for an hour. It thickened into a cream. Then they added vanilla to make it sweet. They put the cream in a large ice chest to keep it cold for days.

People also put toppings on their ice cream. Some broke up cookies and mixed them in. Others added nuts or gummy candies. Many poured melted fudge on top. Soon ice cream was a popular dessert around the world.

Some people grew bored with sweet ice cream. They started to add weird foods to the dessert. People made beef and cactus ice creams. They also used flavors from the sea, such as crab or octopus. One cook made cow tongue ice cream. He mixed red chunks of tongue with vanilla ice cream. Many brave people tried these new flavors.

Today people in Japan eat a special dish called mochi ice cream. It is made up of ice cream wrapped in sticky rice. Each treat is the size of a golf ball. People eat mochi with their fingers instead of a spoon.

From what you pictured...

What is the main idea of the story?

Why do you think only the rich could afford to eat ice cream at first?

Why do you think the servants *raced* back to the palace?

Do you think it was hard to make the first real ice cream? Why or why not?

Do you think more people like sweet ice cream or weird ice cream? Explain.

Do you think many people eat cow tongue ice cream? Why or why not?

54 Musical Sheep Guts

Long ago, people made violin strings out of sheep guts. A string maker got the tube-shaped guts from a butcher. He brought them back to his shop and laid them on a small ramp. He squeezed out the liquid in the guts onto the ramp. The liquid dripped off the ramp and into a wooden tub. Then he soaked the empty guts in cold water.

After the guts had soaked for a few days, the string maker cleaned and inspected them. First he crushed and flattened the tube-shaped guts with a heavy rolling pin. Then he smoothed the outside of the wet tubes with a metal scraper. He looked for holes in each tube. If he found one, he cut the tube where the hole was.

Then the string maker cut and twisted each tube. He inserted a knife into the end of the tube. As he pulled the knife down the side, he sliced the tube into two long strips. He stretched and twisted each strip till it was a thin, strong string. He bundled some strips together to make thicker strings.

Once all the strips were twisted, the string maker hung them out to dry. First he sorted them by thickness. Then he draped each group of strings over hooks on the wall. As the strings dried, they untwisted. So the string maker had to twist each string again and again to keep it tight.

At last, the string maker put four of the dried strings on a violin. He wound them just tight enough to get the right tune. If he cranked them too tight, they would break. He plucked the strings with his fingers to hear their sound. Then he pulled a bow across the strings. They shook back and forth and made beautiful music.

From what you pictured...

What is the main idea of this story?

Why do you think string makers used *sheep guts* to make violin strings?

Do you think violin strings today are made of sheep guts? Why or why not?

Why do you think the string maker squeezed the liquid out of the guts?

Why do you think the string maker smoothed the outside of the tubes?

Why do you think the string maker sorted the strings by thickness?

Do you think the strings would still sound beautiful if the maker had not dried them first? Why or why not?

Index of Stories

Title	Page Number
Argentine Cactus Moth	6
Bad Habit	9
Bajau Seaweed Farmers	19
Carousel Training	21
Couch's Spadefoot Toad	11
Crater of Diamonds State Park	18
Crocodile Bird	18
Dessert on a Stick	3
Dolphin to the Rescue	4
Fairy Pictures	38
Fire Investigator	40
Fishy Snack, A	9
Floating Farms	12
Ghost Picture	27
Giant Squid, The	39
Grass Roofs	7
Great Slide, A	3
Great White Shark on Display	37
Hair Wars	20
In a Tight Space	26
Jai Alai	31
Judge's Hidden Eyes, A	29
Kea Parrots	7
Lights Out in Iceland	28
Mermaid's Purse	30
Mighty Tongue, The	22
Monkey Mail	23
Musical Sheep Guts	44

Title	Page Number
One Helpful Worm	32
Opal Homes	27
Pigeon Race	35
President Arrested	12
Rain Forest Medicine	10
Robot Roach	41
Rotten Sneaker Contest	23
Russian Ice Slide, The	22
Seashell Houses	34
Secret Message Drop, A	8
Shipwreck Homes	4
Singing Finch	19
Sniffing Kiwi Bird	13
Spitting Llamas	11
Sticky Place, A	2
Storm Counting	6
Stuffed Fish Sham	14
Surfing Dolphins	2
Tasty Clothes	28
Tied-up Ox	5
Tiny Bones	15
Tree Bark Make-up	8
Watch Out For Falling Bricks!	14
We All Scream for Ice Cream!	42
Woman's Best Friend, A	36
Worms for Dinner	10

Imagine That! Stories **Color Coding**

The colored checkers along the book's spine represent the grade level of the book. For example, two orange checkers indicate that the book is written at a second-grade reading level. The cream-colored star helps differentiate between volumes at the same grade level.

Production for this book was directed by Jennifer Egan and Michael Sweeney. Illustrations and layout were directed by Valarie Jones, with the assistance of Nury Lee. Back cover illustration by Phyllis Lindamood and Valarie Jones. The Print Editor was Katherine Shields, and the contributing writers were Rachael Burruel, Ben Earl, and Daniel Scott. Manufacturing was directed by David Conway.